LIVING IN THE MOUNTAINS

LIVING IN THE MOUNTAINS

CONTEMPORARY HOUSES IN THE MOUNTAINS

[1] BUILT TO LOOK AT MOUNTAINS

7

[2] BUILT TO BECOME ONE WITH MOUNTAINS

89

[3] BUILT TO CONQUER MOUNTAINS

169

Mountains cover one-fifth of the earth's surface. Rising steeply skywards, inhospitable and often impassable, densely forested or sparsely vegetated, and subject to extreme and changeable weather, landslides, and avalanches, they are some of the most challenging places to live. And yet, nestled in valley floors or perched high on the mountainside, it is here, in the shadows of soaring peaks, that a tenth of the world's population has made its home, drawn by the fertile soil and other natural resources, clean air, or simply the sublime beauty of elevated landscapes.

Architecture evolved from the human need for shelter, the instinctive drive to tame the natural environment. And although residential architecture today is concerned with more than just the practical—providing a refuge from sun, wind, rain, and snow—in the mountains this essential purpose is still a major factor in the design for everything from a rustic mountain hut to the most cutting-edge summit residence. The overwhelming power of the natural world is always evident here, and the need for effective shelter, in addition to beautiful architecture, makes building in the mountains a true test of an architect's abilities.

Despite the significant challenges posed by a sloping, difficult-to-access site, the need for specialized and experienced contractors, and seasonal working restrictions, the mountains are continually used as sites of architectural experimentation. Looking far beyond the vernacular of log cabins and chalets, architects of mountain homes have employed innovative techniques and materials to overcome previous limitations of structure and location—suspending homes vertiginously over steep slopes or else sinking them deep in the rock.

As this book demonstrates, around the world contemporary mountain architecture continues to break new ground, experimenting with form, material, and site. Whether built to appreciate the beauty of the scenery, to become one with the landscape, or to conquer the terrain, these projects pioneer new ways of living in the mountains that—protected by the awe-inspiring topography from the creep of urbanization and interconnectivity—offer a refuge from the modern world as well as the harsh conditions of mountain environments.

This is architecture as adventure, seeking to be tested by the landscape. Even in an era of sophisticated computer modeling and intelligent materials, the mountains continue to be the ultimate proving ground for the architect. Here, in the most extreme and dramatic contexts, bold and visionary questions concerning how and where we live are answered with respect for the same fundamental challenge—to create shelter, to withstand the elements—that has always faced those building in the mountains. This is architecture at its most basic and most complex: life pared back, in communion with the natural world, and exhilarating.

[1] BUILT TO LOOK AT MOUNTAINS

There is something timeless in the beauty of mountain landscapes. Constantly renewed by the changing light, weather, and seasons, mountains are nevertheless resolute and unmoved, cutting the same distinctive form into the sky as they have for millions of years. We see the towering peaks today as the first humans to shelter there did, the same dramatic valleys that for millennia have been worked by hardy farmers, the same tableaux of rock and snow and sky that drew Romantic painters in search of the sublime—the "delightful horror" of the power of the natural world.

Great contemporary architecture is defined more by the experience it creates than its form or function, and the animated permanence of these mountain scenes can elevate beautifully designed domestic spaces to sites of meditation and contemplation. Whereas in previous centuries buildings in the mountains were practical, simple structures with minimal glazing, to prioritize insulation from the cold, modern building techniques have enabled structures to be built high in the challenging terrain and yet be opened to the landscape through high-tech glazing and transitional interior-exterior spaces.

Designing to maximize the views from a particular site demands sensitivity to the environment. The architect has to compose each perspective like a landscape painter, framing the best, most-evocative view before setting it behind glass. It is an art that takes an understanding of when to open the interior to expansive vistas that stretch for miles, and when to create a sense of intimacy, to use focused views—on details of the topography or the local flora —that express the beauty of the mountain on a different scale. As evidenced by the projects in this chapter, when this is successful, the effect is to be immersed in the landscape, to look out and be humbled by the great forces that once thrust the rock into the sky, and gain a wider perspective on our place in the world.

Situated on a vast, empty, high-altitude plain in north-eastern Oregon, the Glass Farmhouse is a residence defined by the expressive landscape that surrounds it. In place of walls, glass panels expose the interior almost completely to the environment—the farmhouse offers privacy for its occupants instead through splendid isolation in eighty acres (thirty-two hectares) of farmland. Blanketed with snow in winter, the home is open on three sides to flat wheat fields ringed by the towering Wallowa Mountains; only the bathroom, study, and storeroom are enclosed at the center of the building. The triple-paned glass facade—which reaches sixteen feet (five meters) on the south flank—is insulated from the harsh Oregon winter with argon gas rather than air and has been designed to benefit from the light and heat captured in cold months while deflecting the high summer sun through the use of an "eyebrow," or "light shelf." The roof, sloping up to achieve this effect, echoes the form of an adjacent wood-frame barn that channels the local vernacular. Inside, the house is minimally appointed, maximizing the space on the relatively restrained footprint, with an open-plan living room and kitchen connected on either side of the house by an open corridor. This residence is conceived as a simple escape into the natural landscape, so artwork and entertainment systems have been eschewed in favor of the ever-changing panorama of land, sky, and mountain.

The soaring views of the Glarus and Grisons Alps from this cabin, isolated on the hillside of a Swiss village, informed the distinctive geometry arrived at by Zurich-based architecture firm OOS. Situated 5,000 feet (1,500 meters) above sea level, the simple structure has been subtly augmented to frame different perspectives of the Alpine landscape afforded by its location. Externally, the monolithic wooden volume mutates in three dimensions, evolving as one moves around the building, and as the large shutters are opened and closed. This design is made possible through the flexibility offered, in planning and construction, by timber. The cantilevered roof of the top-floor terrace—which opens the kitchen-living room space to the exterior and offers a panorama of the landscape—elegantly demonstrates the possibilities of the material.

Internally, the timber structure is exposed, creating a homogenous surface for both interior and exterior and maximizing the building's internal space. The unadorned internal spaces, split over three levels, are accessed by a cascading, irregularly spaced staircase that runs diagonally through the center of the house. This fully enclosed, transitional space—leading from a cellar and garage on the ground floor, to bedrooms and a bathroom on an intermediate level, to the top-floor living area—enhances the impact of the natural light-filled areas and the unique views of the mountains offered by each room.

Lake Maggiore, which stretches some forty miles (sixty-four kilometers) from southern Switzerland into Italy, is a peaceful place of quaint fishing villages and aristocratic palaces built on islands that rise out of the placid water, all surrounded by the vertiginous Alpine landscape. Set into the hillside above the lake, the house, conceived by local firm Wespi de Meuron Romeo, has been designed to maximize the sweeping views across the water to the Alps that soar upwards from the bank opposite. Taking the form of a solid rectangular concrete block emerging from the steep grassy slope, the facade of the building is punctuated with irregularly sized rectangular windows and apertures onto courtyards and terraces, accessed by sliding doors. The structure is further harmonized with its environment through the use of a pale-gray concrete—echoing the color of the local stone—that has been cast using timber boards to leave an imprint of the woodgrain that softens the house's rigid rectangularity with an even rhythm. The rough texture has been alternated with polished concrete surfaces, and the thresholds between various spaces are delineated with stones set into the floor. Sparsely furnished and finished in light wood, the house is at once demonstrative and understated, an assertive minimal design that functions ultimately as a window onto the impressive landscape.

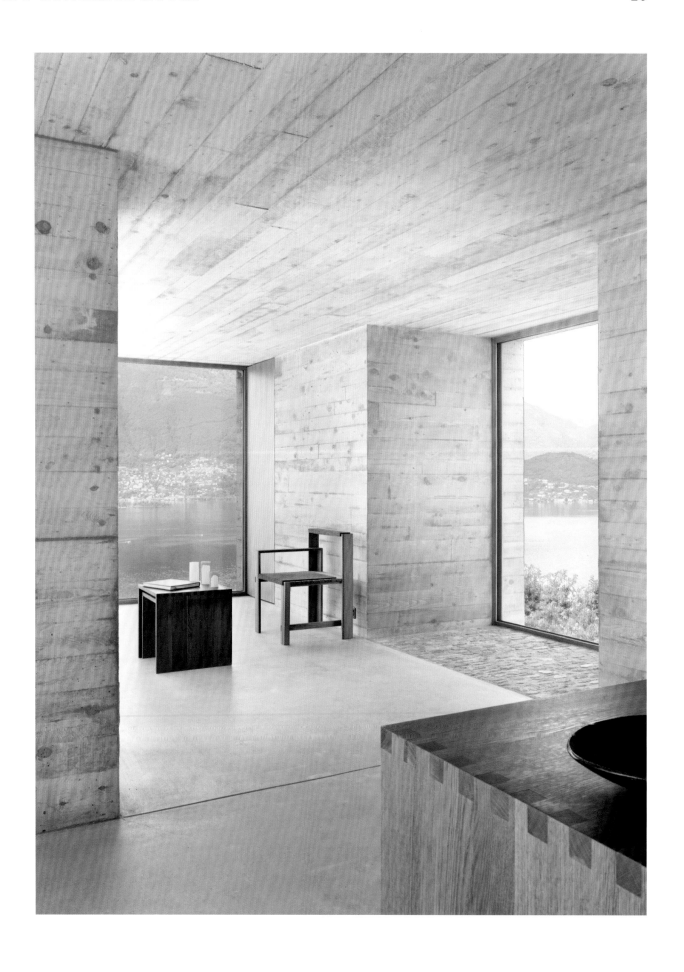

This house, built in the Andes by architects Max Núñez and Bernardo Valdés, is defined by the vast sliding windows at one end of its simple rectangular form. Cantilevered to hang over a steep slope, the thick concrete structure is designed to focus attention on the landscape. The glazing offers a unique perspective across the valley to the mountains that become a dramatic backdrop to the internal space—a library, wardrobe, and bathroom, as well as a minimally appointed bedroom situated immediately in front of the windows to take full advantage of the panoramic views and evening sun.

The intimate feel of the lower level contrasts with the upper, where an airy, fully glazed pavilion houses the living space and leads onto a roof deck that runs the length of the structure, blurring the division between inside and out. From here, views of the higher slopes of the mountain that partially envelops the house, across to more distant peaks and down into the richly forested valley, create a sense of immersion in the landscape. The pavilion, equipped with a kitchen, a table, and chairs, encourages a flexible use of space in conjunction with the exterior deck and pool. With both levels of the house featuring elegantly restrained interiors, this is a residence that has been designed to strip away all but the essentials of modern living to focus on participation in and enjoyment of the breathtaking scenery.

From its vantage point on a sloping site above Lake Gutiérrez in Patagonia, this multifaceted house provides singular views across the lake's limpid waters to the rugged peaks that surround it, and everything about the home's ingenious design enhances the sweeping views. Essentially a collection of "viewing boxes," the house is divided into several volumes that are variously oriented to provide different perspectives of the mountains. Each "box" has floor-to-ceiling windows at one end and is closed down at the other, to draw the eye outward. The volumes are arranged on three levels, graduated in harmony with the slope, allowing unimpeded views on every floor. Clad in local stone, the house imitates its environment to cause minimal visual disruption outside, while interiors are kept white and unadorned so that nothing within distracts from the landscape.

The seemingly disparate volumes are given a sense of cohesion by a terrace that sinuously connects each one to the others and to the outdoors. The house is entered on the uppermost level, which encompasses the living-dining and kitchen area, master bedroom, and guest bedrooms, with children's bedrooms below, and a gym and sauna on the lowest level. An undulating wooden staircase links all three floors. The steep and narrow staircase's stone walls give the impression of a mountain pass, while the fully glazed ceiling ensures a line of sight to the sky and snowcapped mountains is never lost.

LONE MOUNTAIN RANCH HOUSE
2012 | Golden, NM, USA

Set off from the Turquoise Trail, a scenic highway that links Albuquerque and Santa Fe, the Lone Mountain ranch sits low in the high desert of New Mexico. The high-ceilinged, single-story house has been designed to look out at a landscape populated by juniper trees and defined by the mountains that rise from the grassy terrain: Oro Quay Peak, San Pedro, Placer, and Lone. The ranch is named for the latter, visible from the length of Studio Rick Joy's simple rectangular plan; its peak is framed by full-height glazing that opens the kitchen and living space to the outside. A roof terrace, hidden from ground level, offers a complete panorama from the house's isolated position.

The six-bedroom home is part of a 27,000-acre (10,927 hectare) Wagyu cattle ranch that the clients established after traveling to Japan, and a Japanese influence is evident throughout. In addition to the open internal organization that encourages free movement throughout the space, the house uses *yakisugi*, a traditional Japanese method of making wood insect- and weatherproof through charring. Furnished in light, muted tones that echo the surroundings and mindful of sustainability—the twisted hip roof feeds rainwater into a 6,400-gallon (24,200-liter) harvesting system—the Lone Mountain ranch ensures that focus remains on the vast, expansive landscape.

The McDowell Mountains rise monochromatic and resolute out of the desert, twenty miles (thirty-two kilometers) northeast of Phoenix, chameleonic in the changing light. For Chen + Suchart Studio, the challenge was not only to create a residence that benefited from this view but also to obscure the immediate suburban surroundings. As a result, a series of sandblasted masonry walls along the perimeter of the property and an isolated garage clad in weathered steel plate provide privacy for the uninterrupted first-floor space, courtyard, and pool. A dramatic cantilevered mirrored-glass-and-stainless-steel structure has been placed perpendicularly on top, transcending the boundary walls and offering unimpeded views across to the mountains.

These views have informed the internal organization of the space, from the panorama of the landscape that can be seen from the master bedroom and bathroom on the second floor, to smaller, more focused aspects: the guest shower on the first floor with its floor-to-ceiling window, or the perspective of trees, cacti, and mountains framed at the end of a passage between the overlapping external walls, which functions as a transitional space. Polished concrete floors on the ground level reflect the light that flows in through the full-height glazing, which opens the house to the pool, courtyard, and, ultimately, landscape. Together with the balcony that wraps around the upper story, the house's interior becomes a place to look out, to become immersed in the environment without being seen.

The isolated hamlet of Leis sits at 5,000 feet (1,526 meters) above sea level, nestled in the shadow of the Lepontine Alps. In the summer the steep mountainside around the few buildings here is farmed by local families; in winter the slopes run from the ski station at Gadastatt straight past the three timber chalets built by Peter Zumthor. Adapting the traditional Swiss *Strickbau* technique of intersecting planks and with roughly cut slate roofs, the houses are respectful of the local vernacular, but generous glazing—giving views out to the spectacular landscape— provides a contemporary sense of openness. Inside, the timber construction is minimal but warm, and the open-plan top level, containing living, kitchen, and dining areas, is flooded with clear Alpine light. Views become the focus of the house, with each floor and each vantage point offering a new experience of the landscape.

Built initially for Zumthor and his wife as a way to immerse themselves in the Swiss countryside, the first two houses, named the Oberhus and the Unterhus, were later joined by the third, the Türmlihus. Despite the pared-back aesthetic, the houses were an immense technical feat; precise tolerances in the built-in furniture were needed to account for the wooden structure shrinking over time, but ultimately, the scheme has a joyful simplicity.

EFJORD RETREAT CABIN
2017 | Efjord, Norway

Isolated on a ridge on an island in Efjord, this cabin is located deep inside the Arctic Circle; sparsely inhabited and exposed to heavy snow and hurricane-force winds, building and living here can be a challenge. Drawn, however, by the panoramic views across the water to two of Norway's most challenging climbing peaks, the client commissioned Tromsø-based firm Snorre Stinessen Architecture to emphasize the perspectives from the location while ensuring privacy by closing certain aspects of the house to neighboring buildings. To achieve this, two volumes have been offset to create external shelter, while maximal glazing offers expansive views of the landscape from two sides of the single-level living-room structure, which in summer catches the sun from noon until midnight, and from the facade of the two-story volume that houses a bathroom and bedrooms, which also looks out across the roof of the smaller volume.

Externally, the structural glazing has been complemented with aged pine, and the dynamic form—the glass mirroring the changing sky—sinks discreetly into the uneven, rocky environment. Open to the dramatic arctic scenery while creating a sense of comfort and warmth through the birch-clad interior and the use of granite tiles, this is a cabin integrated with the landscape that nevertheless manages to create a sense of privacy and seclusion.

Set on the edge of a protected wilderness in the shadow of the mountains of Chamonix, this chalet draws on a local vernacular of Alpine architecture—a wide overhanging pitched roof and the use of wood and stone—to settle into the landscape. This unassuming form, however, opens up to dramatic views of the surrounding iconic mountain vistas, with the internal layout optimized to offer perspectives of Les Drus and the Aiguille Verte. A generous double-height window ensures that the peaks are visible from both the lounge and a mezzanine above; the glazed walls in the kitchen and window from the basement pool also look out onto the sublime environs.

The architect's careful attention to the home's position in the landscape extends to the materials used, which were chosen after extensive research. The interior of the chalet has been designed to ensure as little as possible detracts from the views. The carefully color-matched recycled wood and the stone sub-basement draw out elements of the environment, while the warm, muted tones of the furnishings have been chosen to complement the scenery. This is a unique, considered design in one of the most sought-after ski locations in the world.

HOUSE IN THE ANDES
2008 | Antioquia, Peru

The simple form of Juan Carlos Doblado's mountain house finds its context in a lush valley encircled by the otherwise dry and arid western slopes of the Andes. Constructed from bare concrete that echoes the stark, crumpled rock rising on all sides of the site, the house's two offset parallel volumes have been positioned to highlight the immediacy and drama of the landscape. Unified by a flat roof, the two volumes create a play of exterior and interior space. Extensive full-height sliding glazing also helps make the environment an integral part of architecture. Large patio spaces, rendered in the same pale concrete, extend out from the house, enclosing a pool and encouraging an active, personal experience of the mountains.

Rising out of the gently sloping ground, the house's utilities are hidden below the main volume, which contains the principal living area, kitchen, and bathroom, while guest bedrooms and a family room are located in the adjacent volume, ensuring that the experience of the main level of the house is fully focused on enjoying the location. With the straightforward, geometric organization and unfussy interior, the structure of the house nearly disappears, bringing the environment to the fore.

In the heavily forested Krokskogen area, architecture firm Atelier Oslo created an intimate refuge that enables enjoyment of the landscape despite the site's challenging conditions. Exposed to strong winds, Cabin Norderhov's cross-shaped footprint helps provide shelter for the exterior spaces, while full-height glass panels in the living and dining areas—the frames hidden—provide a seamless transition to the outdoors. The light, airy interior was designed to optimize views of the terrain; the simplicity of the smooth, contoured birch cladding in the living room, which continues seamlessly throughout, ensures attention is kept on the exterior of the building. Conceived as a continuous space, flowing from living areas to kitchen to bedroom, the interior is centered around a wood-burning fireplace. With the gentle play of levels, following the contours of the slope the cabin is set on, a free use of the space is encouraged: cushions placed on benches along walls and steps offer a variety of vantage points from which to stop and look out. In contrast, the exterior is rectangular and linear, clad in dark-gray basalt slabs that evoke the wooden clapboard of traditional local houses, but which are more durable, emphasizing the cabin as a place of sanctuary from the elements. Almost entirely prefabricated, the cabin was quietly erected using only steel rods embedded in the rock and a small central concrete foundation, causing minimal damage to the environment.

Patagonia, the region at the southern tip of the South America, is one of the least populated areas in the world. With human intervention limited, the landscape is still dominated by the powerful natural forces that created its wide, richly vegetated plains, fjords, and impressive mountain vistas. Rather than attempt to assimilate with the landscape, this house—composed of several asymmetrical geometric volumes—works to draw attention to these dramatic untouched surroundings by emphasizing the contrast between the man-made and the organic. With the scheme thus liberated, each of the five forms, connected by glazed walkways and staircases, has been designed to twist and open independently of the others, creating views on all sides of the site.

The play of exiting and reentering when moving through the smaller glazed spaces between the different volumes continuously rearticulates the house's impression of offering a sanctuary within the often extreme natural environment. In the main spaces, the function of each room determines the level of exposure to the landscape: the double-height living room features floor-to-ceiling glazing, and there are panoramic bedroom windows and smaller openings in the bathroom. Just as the black timber exterior contrasts with the snow in winter, the house is set up as a series of opposing forms that highlight the scenery.

Lying between the Gros Ventre Range and the distinctive Teton mountains, Jackson Hole valley remains largely devoid of human settlement; the uncultivated plains are instead inhabited by the largest elk herd on earth. High on the slopes, looking out on the valley, the winding river, and the brooding mountains, this house, designed by British architecture firm McLean Quinlan, sits discreetly in the landscape. Clad in gray stone that will eventually be covered with lichen, the house has been split into two volumes, which draw from a vernacular of European chalets and wide American cabins. The silvered-cedar-shingle roof also helps the architecture to nestle respectfully within the landscape, justifying its isolated and exposed position that gives the house its defining feature—the dramatic, expansive views.

The heart of the house—the open-plan living, kitchen, and dining room—spans the width of the structure, revealing the gentle rise and fall of the gabled roof. This space can be opened on both sides with sliding glass panels, leading on one side onto decking and a pool. Elsewhere inside, there is a play of scale: smaller spaces, housing a small table or the study, give surprising and focused views of the landscape, drawing out specific aspects of the arresting view, while larger openings, in the children's room and from the bath, allow fuller immersion in the vast, ever-changing surroundings.

LAURENTIAN SKI CHALET
2016 | Saint-Donat, QC, Canada

The Laurentian Mountains in southern Quebec are some of the oldest mountains in the world; formed 540 million years ago, today they are richly forested and a popular rural weekend escape for those working in Ottawa, Montreal, and the city of Quebec. One of the highest residential buildings in the Laurentians, this chalet takes advantage of views that reach for 100 miles (161 kilometers) across the calm waters of Lac Archambault to the peaks of the Mont-Tremblant National Park. Built on pillars sunk deep into the steep slope of a former ski route, the chalet has been raised from the ground, allowing snow and meltwater to move freely beneath the structure and ensuring the topography does not limit the views from the house. A twenty-seven-foot (eight-meter) -long bay window that runs along the top level of the rectangular structure reveals the landscape from every point in the open-plan living space and master bedroom. Throughout the chalet, modern fittings and white walls ensure that nothing competes with the views. The design features timber planks not only on the floor and ceilings but also in details on walls and kitchen surfaces, giving a sense of warmth that references the house's forested environs. An expansive deck extends from the south side of the top floor, so the landscape can be enjoyed from within and without.

Rising dramatically from the wide valley of the meandering Snake River, the Teton Range defines the landscape of this house in east Wyoming. Set into a hill just outside the picturesque town of Jackson, the residence commands a view across the valley to the storied peaks. Built on a plot that the clients had left dormant until they retired, the house represents a place of calm and contemplation, a refuge in which to congregate with the wider family. Balancing spaces that express the drama of the landscape with more intimate views onto closed, planted courtyards, the design conceived by Bohlin Cywinski Jackson encourages meditation through the house's relationship with the natural environment. From the unobtrusive entrance, sited in a gap in the rough concrete wall, the landscape is immediately given visual dominance with a line of sight that runs through the house, from the hall, between two concrete fireplaces, to the fully glazed, cantilevered study. The interior spaces on the main level echo the linear external form of the house and have been divided into wood-clad boxes and glass "pavilions" that mediate between the rugged landscape and the warm and welcoming inner spaces. Below, more open living spaces and a covered terrace encourage a communal experience of the outdoors, completing the varied, resourceful ways the design highlights the majestic mountain scenery.

Set in the shadow of the Rhaetian Alps near the Swiss border, this hillside residence uses the breathtaking views of its environs almost as a part of the architecture itself. The house looks out across a quiet, tree-lined valley and the Adda River to the Bergamasque Alps, and local architect Alfredo Vanotti opened up the whole of one side of the simple raw-concrete structure to the view with high-tech, frameless sliding windows. Following a straightforward and open internal plan in which each room runs the width of the building, and with restrained, functional furnishings, the house presents the landscape as if it were a gallery, a neutral "white cube" that showcases the dramatic surroundings.

Part of a small hillside settlement, with a bell tower that rises over the structure providing a nod to the home's cultural heritage, the building is recessed into the sloping site. A ramp leads down to a discreet courtyard where, through a glazed entrance and an open-plan living room, the mountains are first experienced within the context of the building. A 115-foot (35-meter) -long infinity pool, running parallel to the structure, continues the architectural relationship with the environment, acting as a mirror to the sky and the mountains, abstracting the colors as they shift through the seasons and enhancing the immersive, contemplative experience of the landscape offered by the house.

[2] BUILT TO BECOME ONE WITH MOUNTAINS

Mountains are resistant to change. Despite predictions of great utopian cities in glass and steel rising among storied peaks, the mountains are still largely sparsely populated, continuing to offer isolation and escape from the ever-greater demands of digital, interconnected urban lifestyles. Because of the lack of easy access and other challenges presented by a cliffside location, often only the most hardy people—and adventurous architects— see in the mountains not only a place to live but also an opportunity for total communion with nature.

Architecture that harnesses this connection with its context— that offers a return to the elemental, to rock, snow and sky, the forest and the lakes—can incorporate the atmosphere of its setting into the scheme, making the landscape integral to the experience of the structure. One strategy is to source materials from the local area, settling the building into its surroundings and blurring the division between interior and exterior spaces. The topography can be used to inform the internal organization, echoing the terrain within the scheme. The local architectural vernacular offers a cultural context from which to draw, similarly contributing to softening a building's visual impact. Or a house can be designed to disappear into the mountainside completely, a place to see but not be seen.

While contemporary architecture is today associated with ostentatious displays of scale and form—grand expressions of the architect's sensibility and the engineering innovation that makes them possible—projects like those in this chapter, which become one with nature, demand nuance and understatement. Here the most effective design is quiet, distinguished by what goes unnoticed. The architects minimize the visual and environmental impact of the structure on its surroundings and capitalize on the natural resources of the site. This is architecture that requires focus, care, and an intimate understanding of the environment.

Named for its position in northern Montana—where the Flathead and Swan Rivers run into the crystal-clear waters of Flathead Lake—the small town of Bigfork sits on a plateau surrounded by the Flathead National Forest and the Mission Mountains. Here, half hidden and set back from the shoreline, Stone Creek Camp nestles into the gently sloping site and appears gradually, the various buildings distributed throughout the property. Clad in stained, black cedar and featuring pitched Corten-steel roofs, the gatehouse, three-bedroom guesthouse, and lodge evoke a local vernacular. The main residence, however, seems to emerge from the ground, disguised by a flat, landscaped grass roof and clad with locally quarried granite and reused cordwood, densely packed into rectangular metal frames.

Drawing heavily from the natural world, while remaining refined and contemporary through the use of large glazed surfaces and raw concrete, the main residence creates an immersive experience of nature that is continued in the interior design. Clad with the same cordwood and granite as the exterior, internal spaces are intimate without sacrificing the quality of light —oriented to benefit from the sun throughout the year. The foundations were dug carefully to avoid disturbing the subterranean streams that run beneath the camp into the lake. The architects' thoughtful sensitivity to the home's surroundings results in a true escape into nature.

The oversize concrete walls that extend from Wild Lilac demarcate the different uses of the space and, running east to west, shade the house from the high summer sun—but the walls also work to create distinct views onto the San Bernardino National Forest, within which the structure is set. Rather than offering the same perspective from each space, framing different sections of the landscape encourages a repeated engagement with the house's surroundings. That engagement is aided by sliding floor-to-ceiling glazing that runs perpendicular to the walls, providing a seamless transition to the exterior, where there are landscaped gardens, an indoor-outdoor fireplace, and a pool area. The house is open but restrained, private but offering immediate access to the environment.

Hidden in the foothills of the mountains, the low, discreet volumes hunker into the landscape, and the simple geometry of the scheme possesses an elegant functionality that is animated by its inhabitants and the chaparral and bluish-purple wild lilacs from which the house takes its name. Despite the design's limited visual impact on the environment, the property houses a three-car garage in addition to three bedrooms, four bathrooms, a living, dining, and kitchen space, and a separate pool house. The reserved, unobtrusive design helps the inhabitants relax into the natural world, in a place that is only a short drive from Los Angeles.

Named for the particularly crystalline quality of snow found in this part of the Sierra Nevada mountains in California, the Sugar Bowl Resort was established in the 1930s by Austrian ski champion Hannes Schroll. He drew inspiration from his home town—the medieval village of Kitzbühel—while working with contemporary designers to create the resort, whose timber lodge featured a distinctive sloping roof that would cause snow to slide to the back of the building. Some seventy years later, the area still receives heavy snowfall, and the concept has been reprised by John Maniscalco. Looking to Schroll's lodge and the simple volumes of the historic railroad avalanche sheds found in the area, the architect created a form that is clean and linear, clad in cedar, with steel columns supporting the roof over the second floor. The design has allowed for generous glazing to flood the living spaces and master bedroom suite with natural light, while wood, concrete, and steel create a cozy but contemporary interior. The more closed-off first floor is reserved for the boot room, utilities, and guest and children's bedrooms.

Further accommodating the demands of the site, the structure has been raised above the snow line on a concrete base, elevating the otherwise discreet two-story structure to enjoy glimpses through the surrounding forest to the mountains beyond. Elegant and straightforward, the house assimilates the challenging environment, becoming one with both the mountain and the mountain's architectural history.

The placid turquoise waters of Lake Wakatipu on New Zealand's wild and rural South Island are ringed by the Remarkables, an impressive spine of mountains said to be named for the fact that they are one of two ranges in the world that run directly north to south. Fearon Hay's vacation retreat encourages a flexible use of space, making effective use of the building's small plot. The main bedroom, recessed into the slope on which it sits, opens directly onto the open-plan kitchen-living room and an awe-inspiring panorama of the lake and mountains beyond. Unostentatious and private, the house is hidden from the road and access is gained from a roof concealed beneath gravel. The sides of the reinforced-concrete structure are clad in schist—both materials sympathetic to the building's rugged environment.

The house is minimally furnished in muted tones, allowing views of the landscape to dominate, framed by a forest of beech trees. On two sides of the structure, insulated floor-to-ceiling sliding glass panels grant unimpeded access to the outside in the summer, while underfloor heating and the building's sunken position ensure comfort in the winter. The home sources its water from a nearby stream creating a further connection with nature. The architects have carved out not just a physical space in the mountain, but also a unique perspective on forest, lake, and the stalwart mountains.

CHALET IN SVATÝ PETR

2015 | Krkonoše Mountains, Czech Republic

The gable walls of the traditional chalets in the Krkonoše Mountains—a range that runs between the Czech Republic and Poland—are staggered, with each floor slightly larger than the one below. Conscious of this distinctive technique, Prague-based Znameni Čtyř Architekti conceived a contemporary interpretation of the Krkonoše chalet to replace a building, hidden in the dense forest and gently folding landscape, that had fallen into disrepair. Rising from a granite pedestal, the wooden structure has been faced with artfully positioned red cedar on the gable walls, and the banked copper roof, extending out over the base, maintains continuity with the chalets built here in the past. In addition to enlivening the design, the overhang offers the wooden exterior protection from the elements, prolonging its life and ensuring it weathers slowly.

Drawing on their extensive research into the typology of chalets in the region, the architects also organized the interior with sensitivity to the architectural precedents of the house. The living, kitchen, and dining areas have been situated on the second floor, where there are the largest windows and the most light, while more intimate spaces on the higher levels and below serve as bedrooms and the library. Throughout, the low ceilings accentuate the sense of shelter. Restoring and updating the architectural heritage of the area, using materials that echo the natural surroundings, the house breathes new life into the established vernacular.

Dry and barren in summer, blanketed with thick snow in winter, the vast, high desert of Idaho is a demanding but spectacular place to live. Dwarfed by the landscape and reached by a driveway that is 0.5 miles (0.8 kilometers) long, this house by Olson Kundig revels in its location. The designers opened up the simple, restrained structure to give impressive views across the plains to the Sawtooth Mountains. Designed to be hard on the outside but soft inside, the steel-and-concrete-block structure and walled garden create a place of sanctuary from the strong desert winds. The interior is based around one large, double-height room that functions as a coherent kitchen, living, and dining space, overlooked by a mezzanine bedroom and raised above the snowpack; generous glazing on each wall creates the effect of total immersion in the environment.

Designed for an artist, the house was conceived as a remote live-in studio, and there is a work space on the lower level. The use of durable, low-maintenance materials that allow the exterior to weather the extreme environment is continued inside: unfinished recycled fir for the floors, walls, and cabinets, Carrara marble for the kitchen surfaces, and plaster that uses natural clays and pigments. The house is durable but softened by a muted palette of grays and browns that echoes the environment and ensures that the experience of this outpost is also an experience of the landscape.

ALPINE TERRACE HOUSE
2017 | Wakatipu Basin, New Zealand

Set high on gently sloping land above the Wakatipu Basin in New Zealand's South Island, but dwarfed by the lofty Remarkables mountains, Fearon Hay's house balances delicately in the environment. A simple single-story building of four interconnected structures arranged around a courtyard, the residence has been clad in stained cedar, steel, and darkened stone to sit unobtrusively in the landscape, black and quietly resolute. Subtly cantilevered over its concrete foundation, it appears to float just above the ground. Sliding glass panels that run the length of the structure open out onto a backdrop that is animated by the snow line that rises and falls with the seasons; folding external shutters offer shelter from the high winds common in the area. Fortified from the elements, the planted courtyard offers an oasis of calm, maintaining a connection with the natural world even when it becomes inhospitable.

The continuity of dark colors inside—the walls painted a rich, matte charcoal black—keeps the visual focus outdoors and encourages a straightforward use of space. Lit by the generous floor-to-ceiling windows, the four structures—containing a master suite, two sitting areas, dining space and an open kitchen, a library and reading room, and two guest rooms—allow free circulation through the building. Sleek and refined, Fearon Hay's design pays tribute to its location, celebrating views across the terrain while disappearing into it, hovering quietly like the shadows cast by the mountains above.

HOUSE IN THE MOUNTAINS
2012 | Rocky Mountains, CO, USA

This guesthouse, conceived by New York–based architecture firm GLUCK+, responds to the demands of a client who did not want the untouched view of the Rocky Mountains impeded by a new structure. Sunk into the landscape and camouflaged by a roof "meadow," the house is almost completely hidden in the breathtaking mountain valley. Yet split between two perpendicular, intersecting structures, the two parts of the house accommodate an open-plan kitchen and living space, and three bedrooms and a garage, respectively. The design takes advantage of its inconspicuous position, with both sides of the main living area fully glazed to create a continuous line of sight from a courtyard, through the structure, to the swimming pool on the other side, ensuring that the recessed design does not result in the loss of natural daylight.

The residence is also energy-efficient in many other ways: the green roof provides highly effective insulation; solar walls and panels heat the house, pool, and hot tub during the day, while the floor of the building and the pool function as heat sinks, reducing the need for heating during the night. Though the exterior is largely defined by glass and the grass roof, red, rusted Corten steel is used on the retaining wall and roof fascia to contrast with the verdant tones that otherwise dominate the scheme, playing with the tension between seeing and being seen, man-made environments and the awesome natural landscape.

The untouched forests north of Oslo have long been a refuge from urban life for the city's inhabitants, offering a chance to hike in summer and ski the trails in colder months. Here, half hidden in the landscape, are *hytter*—simply furnished cabins that provide proximity to nature as an integral part of Norwegian culture. Gaining building permits can be difficult, and for the *hytte* conceived for a raised site overlooking Mylla lake, Mork Ulnes Architects had to work within regulations that required a pitched roof. By splitting this traditional form in half, with the four resulting volumes organized on a pinwheel footprint, the designers were able to give each room contrasting views. The two patios formed by the house's plan capture the morning and evening sun, and provide shelter from wind and snow.

While traditional *hytter* often have small, dark interiors, here the untreated-pine-clad structure opens up with generous windows onto the dramatic landscape, and the plywood interior skin is warm in contrast to the winter landscape. A free-flowing interior makes the most of the small footprint, accommodating two bedrooms, a bunk room, two bathrooms, and a kitchen-living room beneath vaulted ceilings that reach to 14 feet (4.3 meters). By innovating with respect to vernacular forms, the architects have incorporated the compact functionality of traditional *hytter* within a contemporary design that suits modern family life. Just as the exterior pine will weather to blend with the snowy landscape, so too will the cabin establish itself within the tradition of Norwegian mountain retreats.

DUST
TUCSON MOUNTAIN RETREAT
2012 | Tucson, AZ, USA

The Sonoran Desert in Arizona receives less than fifteen inches (thirty-eight centimeters) of rain a year but harbors a rich and diverse ecosystem that not only survives in the arid conditions but also has adapted and thrives. Dense fields of cacti and paloverdes cloak the vast desert plains and, in the scheme designed by DUST, have been employed to hide the structure in the landscape. Constructed primarily from rammed earth, the retreat melts into the landscape, the surface of the building responding to the desert light in the same way as the mountain that it is set against.

Within and without, the experience of the house involves the landscape. The parking is hidden 400 feet (122 meters) down a narrow track from the building, necessitating a direct experience of the environment while walking to and from the home. Internal spaces are divided into separate structures, so to move between the living space and the bedrooms, for example, requires traversing the landscape as it changes throughout the day. Close attention has also been given to environmental considerations: the earthen structure provides highly effective insulation; the overhangs offer shade and direct the breeze through the house, which can be fully ventilated with vast sliding doors; and the rainwater-harvesting system provides water for all household uses. The retreat's impact on its environs, both visually and otherwise, is respectfully kept to a minimum, allowing the beauty of the landscape to dominate.

Built over thirty years ago as one of the first residences in the exclusive Red Mountain area of Aspen, this home was originally designed to minimize the impact of the structure on the landscape but was subject to a series of interventions over the subsequent decades. Renovating the building to its former function, Oppenheim Architecture took inspiration from the Japanese philosophy of *wabi-sabi*, which finds beauty in imperfection. The exterior is clad in local stone, weathered copper and steel, and reclaimed wood sourced from the region, which emulate the natural variations, textures, and patterns found in the mountainous landscape.

Inside, the rough grain of the wooden surfaces further echoes the organic expression of the peaks visible through generous windows, and the gray walls and minimal, textured furnishings continue this relationship between the interior and exterior spaces in an intimate domestic scheme. Solar collectors provide power and hot water to the building, reducing dependence on natural resources without impacting the exterior expression of the house. Designed to settle almost imperceptibly into the landscape, the retreat nonetheless provides for an active experience of the environment through generous terraces, with a firepit for winter, and an external dining area and copper plunge pool for use in the warmer months.

WILDCAT RIDGE RESIDENCE
2005 | Aspen, CO, USA

High in the Rocky Mountains, the town of Aspen was one of the first luxury ski resorts in the world, and real estate here remains among some of the most expensive and sought-after in the United States. Where once, however, prestige and taste were expressed through ever-larger and more opulent second homes, today there is a greater emphasis on sustainability. For this home, set away from the main part of town along a ridge—offering striking views of the surrounding Monashee Mountains—Voorsanger Architects conceived a design that restored the site, on which work had already begun for an earlier, abandoned project. The design of the striking two-story structure in sandstone and glass blends in, almost counter-intuitively, with its surroundings. Its impressive folded-plate roof eachoes the craggy peaks of the nearby mountains in both form and colour and, when blanketed with snow in winter, the building all but disappears into the landscape. The home expresses further respect for the environment by its reforesting and rehabilitation of the site.

The architects' consciousness of place and purpose is similarly expressed internally, where a dramatic twelve-foot (four-meter) -long rock wall, rough-hewn and covered in moss, divides the east and west sections of the house. This wall separates the guest bedrooms from the living spaces, study, and master bedroom, which offer a direct perspective onto the dramatic mountains through expansive glazing. With energy drawn from sixty geothermal wells, allowing the house to remain completely off-grid, the Wildcat Ridge Residence is a deliberate intervention in the landscape that nevertheless defers to its context.

Itaipava is immersed in the monumental forms of the Serra dos Órgãos mountain range. The area presents the opportunity to reconnect with nature while still being close to sophisticated restaurants, golf courses, and designer shops—a meeting of landscape and luxury that is evident in Bernardes Arquitetura's design for a couple from Rio and their family. Formed of several distinct volumes that extend alternately into landscaped grounds from a central 197-foot (60-meter) -long corridor, the house sits low in the terrain. The pigmented concrete construction—the result of careful research to match the color of the earth—complements the lush green environment.

The simple geometric design, using either concrete cast with timber or full-height glazing, has been exaggerated: the walls extend out into the gardens to define various domestic spaces exterior to the house, and the vast timber roof stretches to hang over the patios. Together with the uneven edges of the decking, this creates an elegant play on the division between house and environment. The experience of the house, rather than the house itself, becomes one with the spectacular mountains that surround the site on all sides.

LA DACHA MOUNTAIN HUT
2016 | Las Trancas, Chile

For this hut, shrouded in native woodland at the base of the Nevados de Chillán volcanic complex, the architects were guided by sustainability and a sensitivity to the landscape. Set into a steep slope and entered on the second floor, the residence has four levels whose uses were dictated by the position on the hill: the third floor opens up into the partially double-height open-plan kitchen, living, and dining area, offering views across the trees to the mountains. The top-level balcony is accessed using a ladder, while the more intimate lower levels house the bedrooms.

Conscious of the ongoing debate around the consumption of wood and pollution in Chile, the architects conceived a highly insulated structure without reducing the use of glazed spaces, designing the V-shaped plan around a *kachelofen*, a masonry stove used for millennia in Central Europe that stores heat in thick brick walls and requires only one load of wood a day. The structure is oriented to benefit from the path of the sun, maximizing the amount of natural light entering generous windows facing north and west. Sourcing material from the local landscape, the architects clad the hut internally with lingue wood and externally with pine planks, charred on-site using the Japanese *yakisugi* technique to protect them from the elements and avoid the use of chemicals. Borrowing from other cultures while firmly rooted in its immediate context, La Dacha is a harmonious part of the landscape.

HOUSE AT CAMUSDARACH SANDS
2013 | Highlands, Scotland, UK

Taking inspiration from the still-standing Neolithic houses on the Orkney Islands, half-sunk into the earth for protection against the intense storms that blow off the Atlantic, London-based firm Raw Architecture Workshop conceived a house that is integrated into the landscape. Set into steeply sloping land on the rugged northwest coast of Scotland, overlooking mountains to the east and the islands of the Inner Hebrides to the west, the house is defined by these dramatic perspectives. It takes the form of two articulated gabled volumes with floor-to-ceiling windows on both facades that lower in the center to reduce the visual mass of the building and its vulnerability to high winds. With the exception of the exposed-concrete base, externally the house consists of a timber-frame superstructure, painted black to echo the environment—the peat, gorse, and expressive skies—and further lessen its visual impact.

The airy, internal space created by the fully glazed gable ends on the top floor of the house has been used for living areas, with the bedrooms on the floor below, and the entrance hall, boot room, and spare bedroom in the basement, accessed via a staircase lit by a vertical window. Light, scale, and material gently demarcate the interior, moving from darker areas below to the minimal open-plan space at the top of the building, where whitewashed walls and pale wooden floors and cabinets reflect the limited natural daylight at this latitude. This is the perfect place to watch the sun rise behind the mountains and sink beneath the waves in the evening.

The Serra dos Órgãos mountain range, which runs between the Brazilian cities of Petrópolis and Teresópolis, takes its name from its resemblance to a pipe organ. Defining the horizon behind Rio de Janeiro, the distinctive area is a popular retreat for those wanting to escape the bustle and heat of the city for restorative, peaceful nature. Set into the mountainside, encircled by rich jungle, this weekend house serves that purpose for a Carioca couple. Here, in the shadow of distinctive rounded outcrops that appear to swell out of the earth, the main house has been organized along a single level to avoid obscuring the view of the land that rises up on all sides. Only a cantilevered living room, which projects from the principal structure, subverts the simple form. On the exterior and ceiling, louvers of laminated wood are both structural and aesthetic, breaking up the surface of the structure, to reduce its visual impact on the environment, while also protecting the house against the glare of the summer sun. Separate parallel structures include a leisure pavilion, a children's house, and a full spa, which is integrated within the slope of the site. With the utility areas also hidden underground, living and sleeping spaces are focused on absorbing the beauty of the natural environment.

[3] BUILT TO CONQUER MOUNTAINS

In an age when computer-aided design has boosted the ease of creating conceptual, gravity-defying volumes and expressive, organic forms, it is easy to forget that architecture, at its core, is the practice of building. Contemporary architecture—sculptural and sophisticated and ever further from the functional principles of Modernism—does not necessarily reveal its purpose and construction in its form; it is more an art, a visionary manipulation of space and shape, than an expression of architecture as an immensely technical engineering discipline.

In the mountains, however, even the most expressive contemporary structures speak of the challenge evident in their location, of the feat of their construction in isolated, sloping sites and extreme weather. Whether the project is a tiny cabin whose precarious location can only be accessed by helicopter or by foot, or a home composed of a series of volumes that rise from a steeply sloping site on piers driven deep into the rock, the particular requirements of building in the mountains demand a true collaboration between architects, highly skilled engineers, and experienced builders. More than any other terrain, mountains push the technical aspect of the discipline to its limit.

The projects in this chapter not only overcame the particular demands of the terrain, but also reinterpreted what mountain architecture means in the twenty-first century. They explore a vernacular beyond quaint huts and cozy, wooden chalets, while articulating through an ambitious form the triumph of design over arduous conditions. This is architecture that is playful and dramatic, but also conscious and responsible. It justifies its dominant place in the landscape and impact on the environment through sustainable and contextually sympathetic design.

Employing (and sometimes even developing) new techniques and technologies, modern mountain architecture represents the cutting edge of architectural engineering and the greatest challenge to its practitioners. The projects in this chapter demonstrate that the spirit of innovation is alive and well in contemporary architecture.

HOLIDAY HOUSE ON THE RIGI
2004 | Rigi Scheidegg, Switzerland

Surrounded by three vast bodies of water—Lake Zug, Lake Lauerz, and Lake Lucerne—the Rigi is a massif that rises out of central Switzerland to offer panoramic views that stretch for miles. On one of the main peaks of the range, Scheidegg, Zurich-based architecture firm AFGH conceived a vacation home that is perched implausibly on the slope. Set as far as possible from surrounding buildings, the weathered timber structure echoes the winter environment, while its distinctive contemporary volume appears to boast of its challenging location. Organized on a polygonal footprint, the house alludes to the shape of a boat: a chimney rises from the concrete basement that anchors the structure in the landscape, extending from the roof like a mast.

Inside—where the exterior timber cladding has been continued through all internal spaces—the fireplace provides a repeated center of focus over each of the three floors. These differ in the use of space, from a minimally appointed bedroom and bathroom on the top floor to the split-level open-plan living space, where a sixteen-foot (five-meter) -long panoramic window cinematically frames the view across the mountaintops. For the kitchen area, the architects lowered the ceiling to evoke intimate mountain cabins, while at one end of the living area full-height sliding doors open onto an external platform to further benefit from the exposed, elevated position and the awe-inspiring views across the mountain landscape.

Corcovado is a granite peak that towers some 2,310 feet (704 meters) over Rio de Janeiro. The distinctive mountain is known for the 125-foot- (38-meter) -high statue of Christ the Redeemer at its summit and its views across the city to the Rodrigo de Freitas lagoon, Sugarloaf Mountain, and the iconic Ipanema and Copacabana beaches. Sharing a similarly spectacular perspective, the Mata Atlântica Residence, set at the bottom of the cliff that falls away from the feet of the monumental statue, is at once dynamically located in the landscape of rock and tropical forest and yet spacious and relaxed. The house is isolated from the urban setting by its position on the hillside and the landscaped grounds that surround the building. Belying the site's exposed, sloping topography, the design features rigidly horizontal planes running seamlessly from the gardens through the first floor of the house (open on both sides due to full-height glazing) to the decking.

Intimacy has been created by revealing and concealing the view with shutters, and alternating the bright, open-plan rooms with closed interior and exterior spaces. The generous glazing is further supplemented with skylights. With the addition of artwork that further roots the structure in the hillside—a garden sculpture, a mural that contextualizes the house in the landscape—the residence becomes as established on the iconic mountain as the mountain itself is in the city's culture.

The richly forested Yatsugatake Mountains rise suddenly out of the center of Honshu, erupting along the tectonic fault line that divides the country. The landscape inspired Kidosaki Architects Studio to create a design that functions as a viewing platform spectacularly suspended over the sloping topography. The floor-to-ceiling glazing that runs the length of the simple rectangular floor plan yields expansive views over foothills and plains far below. This has a dynamic impact on the internal experience of the house, creating the effect, as the architects say, of "living on a cloud." The impression of weightlessness of the structure is achieved by extending the house from a reinforced-concrete base that roots the building in the mountainside, the cantilevered section supported by two angular struts.

The wooden flooring extends from the open-plan living space to the balcony that wraps around the house, further heightening the sense of continuity between the internal space and the landscape. More intimate, focused perspectives are offered from the bedrooms that face the side of the building. Wood has also been used externally to soften the effect of the impressive structural concrete form in the environment, while the minimal interior ensures the focus remains on the landscape. Having spent years searching for the site, the client discovered in Nagano a place of calm and wonder, now matched by a house that enhances the experience of the surroundings.

The villages built in the lush Sierra Madre Oriental mountains of northern Mexico are defined by the limited usable land in the steep valleys. For P+O Arquitectura, a firm based in the nearby city of Monterrey, modern construction techniques mean the topography of the mountains is not as limiting as it was for those building earlier settlements, though the firm's scheme is nevertheless respectful of the local architectural vernacular and unique ecosystem. Rather than clear the dense cedar trees that surround the site, the architects raised the house above the level of the vegetation, creating striking perspectives of the mountains while minimizing the footprint of the structure. The concrete walls, carefully matched to the warm tones of the local soil, help to integrate the house within the landscape.

Composed of three separate volumes stacked unevenly on top of each other to create open spaces, and cantilevered forms that give changing, focused perspectives on the landscape through full-height glazing, Narigua House encourages a playful discovery of both the surprising internal organization and the home's spectacular location. The main entrance and master bedroom, on the second floor, lead up to kitchen, dining, and living areas lined with timber beams traditional in Mexican architecture. With the mechanical room hidden on the first floor, where the garage and multipurpose guest bedrooms/storerooms are also located, the roof deck is left empty to take in the unimpeded views out across the valley and up the sheer mountain faces that dwarf the impressive structure.

Situated on a terraced site in the foothills of the Himalayas, 6,500 feet (1,981 meters) above sea level, the Woodhouse vacation home by Delhi–based Matra Architects triumphantly takes its form from the backdrop of the highest mountain range in the world. Augmenting the otherwise straightforward rectangular plan, a double-glazed section of the roof rises up to emulate the peaks beyond and opens the interior to the sky. It's a design that emphasizes the effect of weightlessness in the house—the four timber main frames, made from glued planks fastened with steel tie-rods, are able to support the insulated building envelope, a mezzanine level, and the skylight, as well as the timber-clad roof, without the need for supporting columns.

The structure also allows for glazing to run around the floor level of the living area, lifting the house from the stone base on which it was built. Celebrating the environment, both the stone and the warm-toned interior pine cladding were sourced locally and complement the simple but effective trusses that proudly become part of the interior scheme. The focused views from square windows of various sizes in the open-plan living area and the four bedrooms encourage contemplation of peach, plum, and apricot orchards and richly forested surroundings, the sky, and the distant, snow-covered mountains. Reached via a path that leads through the orchards, the house, clad with oiled thun wood, is rooted in the environment and the local vernacular, but establishes a new way of living in the area.

Only a two-hour drive from the cold and wet capital but enjoying a tropical climate, the area around the Colombian city of Girardot is popular with Bogotános looking to escape for the weekend. At Nilo, a small village on the edge of the Santo Domingo plateau, architects Carolina Echeverri and Alberto Burckhardt were given an unusual commission: a pair of vacation homes for two brothers and their families. Here, set into the foothills of the eastern Andes, the architects created two identical structures, which are oriented to optimize the perspectives from each site across the densely vegetated plateau to a lake and the mountains beyond. The designers used the landscape to ensure privacy and isolation for each household without constructing solid boundaries.

With each house, Echeverri and Burckhardt organized the ground floor as a unified social space, where the living area, dining room, and kitchen can be opened by sliding back full-height wooden blinds, giving access to the courtyard and pool, and a separate section with bedrooms that face onto a rock pool. The upper level, accessed via a double-height stairwell that features an aperture to allow palm trees to climb through, offers a more private experience of the landscape, with a balcony and hot tub extending from the master bedroom.

MOUNTAIN CABIN

2012 | Laterns, Austria

The distinctive form of this house designed by Marte. Marte Architects rises from the steeply sloping valley above the Austrian town of Laterns, pale gray and inorganic. Drawing visually from fortified towers, it appears in the landscape as an abstracted, almost pixelated form. The exterior surface of the concrete shell appears rough, evoking the rock it is set into and harmonizing the otherwise strictly linear structure with its context. Stairs lead up to an open level in the center of the building that frames the prominent Alpine landscape in a panorama that introduces a sense of wonder as one arrives at the building.

Inside, the smooth concrete surfaces contrast with the exterior to offer a clear division between the natural world and the minimally furnished interior, enforcing the sensation of fortification and security that defines the scheme. However, natural oak—used for the floor, fixtures, fittings, and thick window frames that asymmetrically dot the facade—warms the living spaces, kitchen, bedrooms, and bathrooms, accessed by a spiral staircase that runs into the basement storage area. Though it dominates the vertiginous site, the house treads lightly on its environment; with the exception of the driveway, the natural form of the terrain has been preserved, and the limited use of materials echoes the austere beauty of the mountain locale.

FRANKLIN MOUNTAIN HOUSE
2015 | El Paso, TX, USA

The Franklin Mountains rise suddenly from the Rio Grande river valley, at the edge of the city of El Paso on the Mexican border, sinking back into the red, dusty earth after running only twenty-three miles (thirty-seven kilometers) north into New Mexico. Isolated on the range's lower slopes, this mountain home looks out over the urban sprawl and across the border to the Mexican desert. The stacked rectangular forms of the house play with their surroundings: the lower level, clad in locally sourced basalt, merges with the spartan landscape; while the upper floor, set perpendicularly on top, and faced with white lime stucco, contrasts with the stark mountainside. Both surfaces consciously draw from the architectural vernacular and culture of the city below, as do smaller details, such as the steel-and-leather doorknobs that evoke the area's connection to the railroad and cowboys. As a result of the steep slope, each floor—from the first level, which houses the residence's utilities; to the second, containing the living, kitchen, and dining areas; to the third, with bedrooms and family room—exits directly to the outdoors. The house is sited on a series of terraces that allow native flora to flourish, and the succulents, grasses, and cacti that surround the plot attract deer and rabbits. Taking inspiration from the pieces of quartz that stand out on the mountain, discarded from the abandoned mine close by, this is a sanctuary that triumphantly asserts itself within its setting.

Sited in an area of the French Alps with restrictive architectural guidelines, this mountain chalet is the product of careful research into the historical typology of buildings in the region. Respectful of the prescriptive height, width-to-roof-slope ratio, and window sizes, the scheme proposed by Parisian architecture firm Studio Razavi subtly updates the architectural heritage, bringing the mountain chalet into a contemporary context. The simple ground level, made of concrete cast using timber planks that evoke the external cladding of the house, contains an open garage and room with a stone floor to change into ski gear; the bedrooms and open-plan living area are located on the second and third stories, respectively. Taking inspiration from the original functional organization of Alpine houses, where animals were kept on the first floor, fodder on the next level, and the living spaces at the top, here the levels of the structure are used to create a sense of progression, ascending through the house to lighter, more open spaces, culminating in a living space with full-height glazing and a balcony giving views across the mountainous landscape and ski routes.

In a response to the tendency for pastiche and unnecessary decorative elements in newly built chalets, the Mountain House has been stripped back to the essentials, eschewing ornament and limiting internal decoration to a measured use of tile, painted surfaces, and fabric. In this way, the house is closer to traditional mountain architecture than many of the chalets with which it was required to assimilate.

Set into a sloping pasture in Brenna, this modern barn was designed as a countryside residence for the head architect of KWK Promes. Isolated within a vast landscape of rolling hills and the mountains of Brenna, the design was informed by the site, evolving with each new challenge from the environment. The home was initially conceived as a simple, single-story barn; the landslides common in Polish mountains led the architect to raise the structure off the ground, allowing water to move freely beneath. Concerns about security, because of the remote location, led the house to be twisted so that only one corner touches the ground. This became the entrance, accessed by a drawbridge which, when raised, acts as a shutter. Along with the thirty-three-foot (ten-meter) -long sliding concrete wall, it creates a sense of solidity and impregnability. With no need for a perimeter wall, there is uninterrupted access to the landscape.

Complying with local planning regulations as well as the vernacular of mountain architecture, the gable roof gives the structure an unassuming, appropriately agricultural appearance, which has been made contemporary by the use of simple, light gray concrete. With panoramic views enabled by the full-height glazing that runs the length of the house—from the open-plan living area to the sleeping and bathroom spaces—this is a structure that celebrates its challenging position on the hillside.

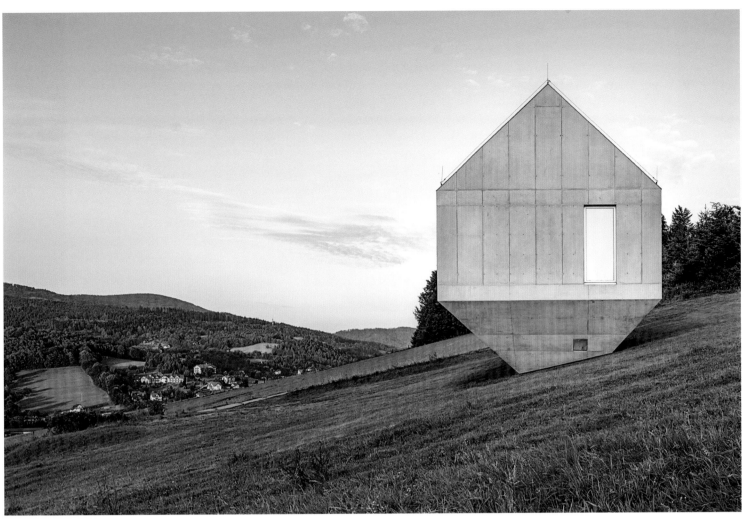

For centuries the particular quality of light in the Swiss village of Maloja at the western end of Lake Sils has drawn painters to this area of distinct natural beauty. It's in this unique Alpine climate that shoe brand On built a mountain refuge nearly 8,200 feet (2,499 meters) up Piz Lunghin, the mountain known as the "Roof of Europe," with views across the valley where the company was started. Only accessible by a two-hour hike over demanding terrain, overcoming the considerable challenges faced by its isolated and elevated position, the On hut is a feat of engineering. The wooden construction, plywood interior, and reflective corrugated-metal exterior keep weight to a minimum while ensuring that the project is sustainable and leaves no trace on the mountain.

Despite its small footprint, the hut is remarkably well appointed, with solar panels providing power for the lights and charging mobile phones, and a unique rainwater-harvesting system that supplements water that can be collected from a nearby glacial spring. Inside, the hut is simple and efficient, the stepped floor, reflecting the slope of the site, demarcating the different uses of the open space—from the vast, full-height glazing that leads from a small balcony to a living area, with a table and seating, to a wood-fired stove used for heating and cooking, to a wet room, from which a toilet, wardrobe, and cupboard can be accessed; a mezzanine, reached via a ladder, gives even more elevated views of the stunning scenery.

At once echoing the peaks of the Elk mountain range that this vacation home is set within and representing a striking intervention in the landscape, the house at Owl Creek was built as a place for the client's family and friends to congregate close to the celebrated ski resort at Snowmass in Colorado. The retreat is clad in weathered steel to echo the color of the mountains in warm months and firmly anchored in the hillside. The house's position necessitated a triangular footprint in order to maximize the amount of natural light entering the internal spaces. This effect is intensified by double-height glazed walls, which offer an uninterrupted view out to the mountains beyond.

The house's triangular form continues as a motif throughout the building, from the cantilevered terrace that extends from the airy, split-level communal area, to the lower levels that create a more private atmosphere for the five bedrooms; a steam room and hot tub with panoramic views of the landscape are also located there. The angular forms bring a dynamism to materials that quote from the house's surroundings: the stacked-stone columns evoke the banks of nearby Owl Creek and the local aspen trees. Designed to be used year-round and by several families at once, Skylab's direct response to the area's topography creates a dramatic and yet welcoming space to come together and experience the environment.

Situated at the summit of a hill and blissfully secluded, this hut was designed as a vacation retreat. From its elevated position looking out across the rolling hills and the Murrumbidgee River, the hut has a commanding perspective, which is showcased through extensive glazing. The straightforward A-frame construction takes inspiration from the basic form of a tent, and the beams that support the corrugated-metal roof visually and physically anchor the cabin in the ground. Reached via a walkway, the entrance immediately re-emphasizes the sweeping perspective afforded by the site's location: windows draw the eye and give way onto the fully glazed end wall and decking that extends seamlessly from the interior floor. The cabin's internal space is defined by the living-sleeping area and is equipped with a shower and small cooker, while a barbecue and wood-fired hot tub encourage outdoor living.

Though the cabin's position is visually prominent, the design nevertheless has a minimal environmental impact. Built from locally sourced, sustainable hardwoods, the structure was assembled on-site by a two-person team, minimizing the need for intensive construction processes, and power is drawn from solar panels. With wood-burning stoves providing heat for both the cabin interior and the hot tub outside, the hut offers a completely off-grid experience that immerses its inhabitants in the vast, picturesque landscape.

Rising through dense forest to command views of the Mexican city of Monterrey, Tatiana Bilbao's design for a family home has been informed by the restrictions of the site. The house is set into a steeply sloping hillside, and the structural complexity of building on the exposed plot demanded the use of concrete. This has been used to construct a series of intersecting angular volumes, loosely based on the form of a pentagram, arranged on a geometric plan. When viewed within the landscape, these pale, asymmetric volumes suggest an organic form, such as an exposed cliff face. The play of levels integrates the building into the landscape and gives the impression that the house has grown out of the undulating ground. The multilevel design also satisfies the client's request for a division between public and private areas. An open-plan living area creates a sense of expansiveness through floor-to-ceiling glazing that belies the weight and solidity of the structure. More intimate spaces are accessed via a spiral staircase.

Taking inspiration for the form of the house from mid-century Modernist homes built in the Hollywood Hills, Bilbao's Mexico City studio has created a clean, warm, homogenous interior that features the use of black sabino wood for wall cladding, shelving units, and floor tiles that run throughout the space. The wood incorporates texture and the surrounding environment into a scheme otherwise dominated by austere, smooth concrete surfaces and, ultimately, the staggering views of the city and sublime natural landscape.

Situated on a small exposed plateau, 3,937 feet (1,200 meters) above sea level amid the mountains and glaciers of northern Norway, the Rabot Cabin's isolated locale is only accessible by foot—building materials had to be delivered to the site by helicopter. To meet the demands of the location, the architects conceived a form that was compact and hidden from the elements, and gave particular consideration to the materials used: specially calibrated glass for the vast, full-height windows and thick locally sourced timber boards, aged using ferric sulfate so the structure appears gray, softening its visual impact in the landscape.

Taking its name from the French glaciologist and geographer Charles Rabot, who explored the mountains extensively, the cabin is the most remote of the Norwegian Trekking Association refuges. The plan is centered on a communal kitchen that sits beneath a spacious mezzanine, opening on either side to two double-height common rooms, flooded with natural light, that look onto the mountains and the valley below, respectively. Heated by wood-burning stoves, each area can be closed off with sliding doors when not in use, for more efficient heating in a location where resources can be in short supply. Without connection to the power grid, electricity for the lights is drawn from solar panels. A refuge in the rugged, undulating landscape, the cabin is open and contemporary, while able to weather the worst the inhospitable environment can throw at it.

Echoing imposing, impenetrable hilltop castles of the Middle Ages, Villa E, by architects Olivier Marty and Karl Fournier of Studio KO, perches defiantly atop an isolated ridge in the foothills of the Atlas Mountains. The house's form, from a distance, is monolithic and simple: a vast block of local ocher stone that is revealed on closer inspection to be composed of roughly hewn bricks of varying sizes. In a design that is attuned to the landscape and local vernacular, Moroccan craftsmanship in the textiles and furnishings, as well as muted earth tones, soften a minimal, contemplative scheme that plays subtly with the texture and malleability of materials.

Wood, dark stone slabs, and white marble are used alternately on the floors throughout, and the walls are concrete or whitewashed or clad with panels of irregular thin wooden planks. This focus on the tactility of the interior creates an intimacy that balances the house's exposed position, and views from the house to the vast surroundings are controlled, limited to small square apertures in the wall, positioned to maximize airflow through the building. Sunlight is used sculpturally, flowing in through thin gaps in the walls or high windows in the bathroom. Where the landscape is seen, floor-to-ceiling windows open suddenly onto dramatic and unimpeded perspectives across the Ourika River valley to the mountains, framing a view of the highest peak in the Atlas Mountains, Mount Toubkal.

Pezo von Ellrichshausen
SOLO HOUSE
2012 | Cretas, Spain

At the summit of the Tossal dels Tres Reis, a mountain that rises out of the Catalonian countryside, there is a cairn that marks the meeting place of three ancient Spanish kingdoms, Catalonia, Valencia, and Aragon—according to legend, three monarchs met here to agree on the boundaries of their territories. This fabled site forms part of the Ports de Tortosa-Beseit massif, and the backdrop to Pezo von Ellrichshausen's experimental Solo House. Rising from a two-story podium shrouded in tall, dark-green trees, the bare concrete form appears weightless in the landscape. Designed on a rigidly square footprint and organized around a central courtyard with a pool, the scheme plays with the divisions between interior and exterior. The four pine-clad rooms on each side of the house are open to the landscape and balconies on each corner through full-height glazing, taking advantage of the structure's dominant and isolated position.

Solo House was the first of a series of residences to be built in the area as part of a project that gave twelve avant-garde architects complete freedom in their designs. Bringing a geometric simplicity to the concept of a second home, the structure's minimal approach reaches its purest expression in the courtyard. With the exception of focused views into the landscape through a single doorway, the courtyard celebrates the house's prominent position only through the changing sky as the sun moves across the gray ceramic tiles that line the walls.

INDEX

Page references for illustrations appear in **boldface**.

Phaidon Press Limited
2 Cooperage Yard
London E15 2QR

Phaidon Press Inc.
65 Bleecker Street
New York, NY 10012

phaidon.com

First published 2020
© 2020 Phaidon Press Limited

ISBN 978 1 83866 084 0

A CIP catalogue record for this book is available from the
British Library and the Library of Congress.

Commissioning Editor: Virginia McLeod
Project Editor: Emma Barton
Production Controller: Abigail Draycott
Design: SJG/Joost Grootens, Dimitri Jeannottat,
    Julie da Silva
Text: George Upton

Printed in China

The publisher would like to thank Jamie Ambrose, Sarah
Bell, Vanessa Bird, and Lisa Delgado for their contribu-
tions to the book.